TEAM SPIRIT ®

SMART BOOKS FOR YOUNG FANS

THE SEATTLE MARINERS

BY
MARK STEWART

NORWOOD HOUSE PRESS

CHICAGO, ILLINOIS

Norwood House Press
P.O. Box 316598
Chicago, Illinois 60631

For information regarding Norwood House Press, please visit our website at:
www.norwoodhousepress.com or call 866-565-2900.

All photos courtesy of Getty Images except the following:
Black Book Partners Archive (6, 7, 10, 11, 17, 21, 22, 23, 28, 34 bottom right,
35 top left & right, 37, 40, 43 both, 45), Tom DiPace (8, 14, 35, 36, 39),
Topps, Inc. (15, 33, 34 top & bottom left, 41, 42 top & bottom left), Matt Richman (48).
Cover photo: Otto Greule Jr/Getty Images

The memorabilia and artifacts pictured in this book are presented for educational and informational purposes,
and come from the collection of the author.

Editor: Mike Kennedy
Designer: Ron Jaffe
Project Management: Black Book Partners, LLC.
Special thanks to Topps, Inc.

Library of Congress Cataloging-in-Publication Data

Stewart, Mark, 1960-
    The Seattle Mariners / by Mark Stewart. -- Library ed.
        p. cm. -- (Team spirit)
    Includes bibliographical references and index.
    Summary: "A Team Spirit Baseball edition featuring the Seattle Mariners
that chronicles the history and accomplishments of the team. Includes access
to the Team Spirit website, which provides additional information, updates
and photos"--Provided by publisher.
    ISBN 978-1-59953-497-8 (library : alk. paper) -- ISBN 978-1-60357-377-1
(ebook) 1. Seattle Mariners (Baseball team)--History--Juvenile literature.
I. Title.
    GV875.S42S74 2012
    796.357'6409797772--dc23
                                            2011048203

Manufactured in the United States of America in North Mankato, Minnesota.
196N—012012

9460

COVER PHOTO: The Mariners can't wait to celebrate a 2009 victory.

TABLE OF CONTENTS

ABOUT OUR GLOSSARY

In this book, there may be several words that you are reading for the first time. Some are sports words, some are new vocabulary words, and some are familiar words that are used in an unusual way. All of these words are defined on page 46. Throughout the book, sports words appear in **bold type**. Regular vocabulary words appear in ***bold italic type***.

MEET THE MARINERS

The **Pacific Northwest** draws sports lovers from all over the country—and from all over the world. In this corner of the United States, people can do fun activities in the woods, on the water, and in the mountains. The Seattle Mariners are an important part of that picture, especially during the spring and summer.

The Mariners have a wonderful way of finding players with unusual talents. Seattle might sign a star from a foreign country. Or the "M's" may trade for a good young player from another club. Either way, they know how to put together an exciting team.

This book tells the story of the Mariners. While they are only one part of the Seattle sports landscape, they play a big role when it comes to bringing sports lovers together. Indeed, when the Mariners are winning, they are the hottest ticket in town.

Ichiro Suzuki—known throughout baseball by his first name, Ichiro— helped the Mariners become popular with fans all over the world.

5

GLORY DAYS

Baseball has a long history in Seattle. A team in the **minor leagues** called the Rainiers played there for many years. In 1969, the city was awarded its first big-league team, the Pilots. Unfortunately, Seattle wasn't quite ready. Its stadium was old and small. The Pilots moved to Milwaukee after one season and became the Brewers. Meanwhile, Seattle began preparing to host another baseball team.

That day came in 1977, when the Mariners arrived in town. They built their team with unwanted players from other clubs. They added promising young players from high school and college in the **draft**. The Mariners moved into a new stadium called the Kingdome. They shared it with the Seattle Supersonics basketball team and Seattle Seahawks football team.

The Mariners continued to search for players who had been overlooked by other teams. In their early years, their hitting stars included Ruppert Jones, Ron Fairly, Dan Meyer, Leroy Stanton, Bruce Bochte, Leon Roberts, Willie Horton, Ken Phelps, and Al Cowens. Their best pitchers were Glenn Abbott, Rick Honeycutt, and Bill Caudill.

In the mid-1980s, Seattle welcomed a group of homegrown stars. The best was Mark Langston, a left-handed pitcher who led the **American League (AL)** in strikeouts as a **rookie**. First baseman Alvin Davis, second baseman Harold Reynolds, third baseman Jim Presley, and outfielder Phil Bradley formed the core of a solid offense.

Even with this talent, the Mariners did not have their first winning season until 1991. By then, they were building a new team around an

amazing young outfielder named Ken Griffey Jr. He would lead the AL in home runs four times and win 10 **Gold Gloves**.

Randy Johnson also joined the Mariners during this time. He was a tall left-handed pitcher who whipped the ball in at terrifying speeds. Johnson pitched Seattle's first **no-hitter** in 1990 and led the AL in strikeouts four years in a row. Other Seattle stars during this time included Edgar Martinez, Jay Buhner, Tino Martinez, and Alex Rodriguez.

The Mariners found a great manager to lead these players in Lou Piniella. He guided the team to the **American League Championship Series (ALCS)** twice, but both times Seattle fell short of winning the

LEFT: Ken Griffey Jr. gave fans a lot to smile about during his 13 seasons in Seattle.   **ABOVE**: Randy Johnson became baseball's best left-handed pitcher with the Mariners.

pennant. In 1998, the Mariners began looking in a new direction. Johnson was traded, and then Griffey was traded, too. A year later, the team opened a brand-new ballpark. When Rodriguez left Seattle after the 2000 season, even the most loyal fans wondered when the Mariners would have a good team again.

No one expected Seattle to be *competitive* when the 2001 season began. However, the Mariners had more talent and pride than anyone had imagined. They also had Ichiro Suzuki, a Japanese baseball star playing his first season in North America. Ichiro was so famous in Japan that he went by just one name. Seattle fans continued this *tradition*.

And why not? Ichiro was sensational. He led the AL in hits, stolen bases, and batting average in 2001. Bret Boone batted .331 and drove in 141 runs. Jamie Moyer, one of the oldest pitchers in baseball, won 20 games for the first time in his life. Freddy Garcia also had a great year on the mound and was named an **All-Star**. The Mariners amazed the baseball world when they set an AL record with 116 wins.

In the years that followed, new players took the field for Seattle, including Raul Ibanez, Richie Sexson, Adrian Beltre, J.J. Putz, and Felix Hernandez. As the team looks forward, it also looks back to the 2001 club for the winning formula: Play hard, play smart, and play to win.

LEFT: Ichiro   **ABOVE**: Freddy Garcia

HOME TURF

The Mariners' first home was the Kingdome. The stadium protected fans and players from rainy weather, which occurs often in the Pacific Northwest. For many years, the Kingdome's 23-foot right field wall was the second-highest in baseball.

In 1999, the Mariners opened a new ballpark. It has a *retractable* roof made of three panels, which slide into place when rain is in the forecast. An interesting feature of the stadium is that it is not totally enclosed when the roof is shut. Air flows through the sides of the building, so fans inside feel like they are still outside. The roof is incredibly strong. It can absorb lightning strikes, hold more than six feet of snow, and withstand winds up to 70 miles per hour.

BY THE NUMBERS

- The Mariners' stadium has 47,116 seats.
- The distance from home plate to the left field foul pole is 331 feet.
- The distance from home plate to the center field fence is 405 feet.
- The distance from home plate to the right field foul pole is 326 feet.

The roof is open and fireworks are popping at the Mariners' stadium.

DRESSED FOR SUCCESS

Seattle is one of the largest port cities in North America. When the Mariners first announced their name, fans were happy that it linked the team to the sea. For Seattle's first 10 seasons, the *M* in Mariners was formed by the three points of a **trident**. According to legend, the spear belonged to Neptune, an ancient god of the sea. The team colors were blue and yellow.

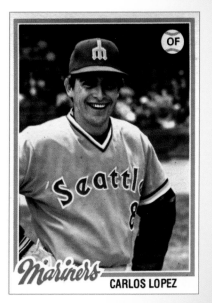

OF

CARLOS LOPEZ

In 1987, the Mariners stopped using the trident design and switched to a yellow *S* on their caps. In 1993, the team started using a design featuring the points of a compass. This **logo** represents the sea, technology, and the great outdoors. Each is an important part of life in the Pacific Northwest.

Seattle's colors are navy blue, silver, and dark green. The team plays in white uniforms at home and gray ones on the road. On special days, they sometimes wear navy blue or dark green jerseys.

LEFT: Chone Figgins runs the bases in Seattle's 2011 road uniform.
ABOVE: Carlos Lopez wears the team's old trident hat.

WE WON!

The Mariners played their first 14 years without having a winning season. In 1991, the team finally won more games than it lost, but still finished fifth in the **AL West**. It took four more years before Seattle could claim its first division crown—but as any Mariners fan will tell you, it was worth the wait.

For most of the 1995 season, it looked as if the Angels would win the AL West. They built a big lead over the Mariners, partly because Seattle lost Ken Griffey Jr. for 90 games with a broken wrist. Fortunately, the hitting of Edgar Martinez and pitching of Randy Johnson kept the Mariners close in the standings. When "Junior" returned, the Mariners were able to catch the Angels.

The teams played one final time to decide who would go to the **playoffs**. Manager Lou Piniella picked Johnson to start this important game. Johnson had led the AL in strikeouts and **earned run average (ERA)** that season. He pitched a masterpiece against the Angels, and the Mariners were AL West champions.

The Mariners then met the New York Yankees. The first team to win three games would play for the pennant in the ALCS. The

Edgar Martinez got several big hits for the Mariners in the 1995 ALCS.

Yankees won the first two games. Suddenly Seattle had its back against the wall.

Johnson beat the Yankees in Game 3. The Mariners also won Game 4, 11–8. Martinez was the hitting hero, with seven **runs batted in (RBIs)**. Game 5 was one of the most tense and hardest-played games in baseball history. The fans in the Kingdome were on the edge of their seats all night.

The Yankees built a 4–2 lead, but the Mariners tied the score in the eighth inning. The Yankees loaded the bases in the ninth inning with no outs. Piniella called Johnson into the game. The exhausted pitcher faced three of baseball's toughest hitters—Wade Boggs, Bernie Williams, and

Paul O'Neill—and got a strikeout and two pop-ups to save the day.

The Yankees scored a run in the 11th inning to take a 5–4 lead. Once again, the Mariners found themselves facing the end of their season. At this point, they simply refused to lose. Joey Cora reached first base safely on a bunt, and then Griffey lined a single to center field. The next batter, Martinez, smashed the ball over third base and into left field. Cora scored easily. Griffey, running faster than he ever had in his life, rounded second base and looked into the eyes of the third base coach, Sam Perlozzo. Both men knew that there was no way Griffey was stopping—he was going to score. He slid into home plate ahead of the throw, and the Mariners came rushing out of the dugout to celebrate the winning run. It was—and still is—the greatest moment in team history.

ABOVE: Ken Griffey Jr. slides home with the winning run against the New York Yankees in Game 5.
RIGHT: Griffey finds himself at the bottom of a pile of happy Mariners.

GO-TO GUYS

To be a true star in baseball, you need more than a quick bat and a strong arm. You have to be a "go-to guy"—someone the manager wants on the pitcher's mound or in the batter's box when it matters most. Fans of the Mariners have had a lot to cheer about over the years, including these great stars …

 ## THE PIONEERS

JULIO CRUZ   Second Baseman

• BORN: 12/2/1954   • PLAYED FOR TEAM: 1977 TO 1983

Julio Cruz was the man who made the Mariners go in their early years. He stole 290 bases for Seattle—including 32 in a row from 1980 to 1981. When he retired, he held the team record for steals.

PHIL BRADLEY   Outfielder

• BORN: 3/11/1959   • PLAYED FOR TEAM: 1983 TO 1987

Phil Bradley was one of the top left fielders in baseball when he played for the Mariners. He was also a good hitter. Bradley batted .301 during his five seasons in Seattle.

RIGHT: Edgar Martinez

MARK LANGSTON   Pitcher

- BORN: 8/20/1960 • PLAYED FOR TEAM: 1984 TO 1989

Mark Langston overpowered hitters with a blazing fastball. He led the AL in strikeouts three times, including his first season. Only three other rookies had done that before.

ALVIN DAVIS   First Baseman

- BORN: 9/9/1960 • PLAYED FOR TEAM: 1984 TO 1991

Alvin Davis had a powerful swing and a sharp batting eye. In 1984, he became the first Mariner to win a major award when he was named **Rookie of the Year**.

EDGAR MARTINEZ   Designated Hitter/Third Baseman

- BORN: 1/2/1963
- PLAYED FOR TEAM: 1987 TO 2004

Many fans believe that Edgar Martinez was the best hitter in team history. In 18 seasons, he had 514 doubles and 1,261 RBIs. He won the AL batting crown twice.

JAY BUHNER   Outfielder

- BORN: 8/13/1964
- PLAYED FOR TEAM: 1988 TO 2001

For many years, Jay Buhner was the "glue" that held the Mariners together. He was a great team player and the first Mariner to hit 40 home runs three years in a row.

KEN GRIFFEY JR.   Outfielder

• BORN: 11/21/1969   • PLAYED FOR TEAM: 1989 TO 1999 & 2009 TO 2010

Ken Griffey Jr. was the best all-around player in baseball when he wore a Seattle uniform. Junior led the AL in home runs four times from 1994 to 1999, and hit 56 home runs two seasons in a row. He was also the best defensive outfielder in the league.

RANDY JOHNSON   Pitcher

• BORN: 9/10/1963

• PLAYED FOR TEAM: 1989 TO 1998

At nearly seven feet tall, Randy Johnson was the tallest player in baseball when he pitched for the Mariners. The "Big Unit" threw the team's first no-hitter in 1990 and won the **Cy Young Award** in 1995.

BRET BOONE   Second Baseman

• BORN: 4/6/1969

• PLAYED FOR TEAM: 1992 TO 1993 & 2001 TO 2005

The Mariners traded Bret Boone away when he was just 24, and then finally got him back seven years later. In 2001, he rewarded them by having one of the greatest seasons ever by an AL second baseman, with 206 hits, 37 home runs, and 141 RBIs.

ALEX RODRIGUEZ   Shortstop

• BORN: 7/27/1975   • PLAYED FOR TEAM: 1994 TO 2000

When Alex Rodriguez hit .358 in 1996, it was the highest batting average ever by a player who started a season younger than 21. "A-Rod" became an excellent power hitter, fielder, and baserunner during his years with the Mariners.

ICHIRO   Outfielder

• BORN: 10/22/1973   • FIRST YEAR WITH TEAM: 2001

Only a handful of players have been named the Rookie of the Year and **Most Valuable Player (MVP)** in their career. Ichiro won them both in his first season with the Mariners. In 2004, he used his slashing swing and great speed to set a new record with 262 hits in a season.

FELIX HERNANDEZ   Pitcher

• BORN: 4/8/1986   • FIRST YEAR WITH TEAM: 2005

When 19-year-old Felix Hernandez joined the Mariners, he already looked like an experienced star. He could throw his fastball and curveball to every part of the strike zone, and he was very cool under pressure. "King Felix" won 19 games in 2009 and took home the Cy Young Award the following season.

LEFT: Bret Boone   **RIGHT**: Felix Hernandez

CALLING THE SHOTS

The Mariners have always had their most success with a roster that mixes experienced players with up-and-coming stars. The *veterans* serve as teachers for their teammates. The young players give the team a boost of energy. Keeping everyone focused on winning is the job of the manager.

Seattle's best managers have commanded the respect of the veterans and worked on the basics with the rookies. Jim Lefebvre led the Mariners to their first winning season, in 1991. He was a star player in the 1960s. Mike Hargrove was also a star during his playing days. He was very good at helping the Mariners stay relaxed and focused. But in 2007, Hargrove proved just how tough managing can be. He left the team right in the middle of a winning season. He was exhausted!

Lou Piniella was the best manager the Mariners ever had. Piniella was anything but relaxed. As a player, he often lost his cool. When he became Seattle's manager, the players learned that they better play

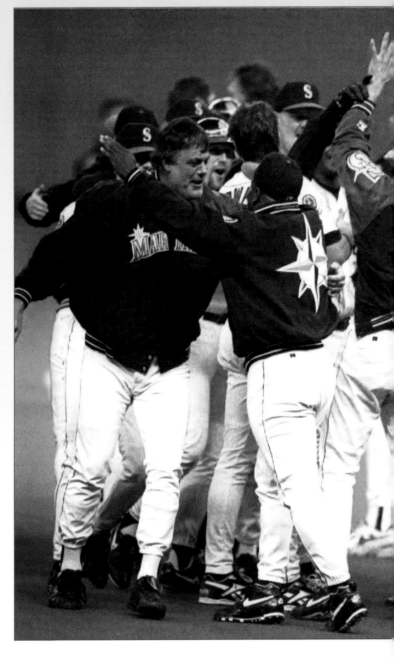

Lou Piniella joins in the celebration after Seattle's win over the New York Yankees in the 1995 playoffs.

hard all the time. Otherwise, "Sweet Lou" wouldn't be so sweet anymore!

Piniella demanded the best from the Mariners, and he usually got it. After being hired in 1993, he led the team to its first four trips to the playoffs. In 1995, the Mariners beat his old team, the New York Yankees, for their first-ever playoff victory.

Piniella guided Seattle to four seasons with more than 90 victories. His greatest achievement came in 2001. That year the Mariners won 116 games.

ONE GREAT DAY

Hitting a home run takes skill, strength, and perfect timing. It also takes a little luck. Think about how hard it would be for one player to hit four home runs in the same game. Before Mike Cameron and the Mariners took the field against the Chicago White Sox on a spring evening in 2002, only three American Leaguers had ever done this. Cameron would soon become the fourth.

In the first inning, Cameron swung at a fastball from starting pitcher Jon Rauch and hit it out of the park. Later in that same inning, Cameron came up again against relief pitcher Jim Parque—and hit another ball over the fence! Seattle's second baseman, Bret Boone, also hit two home runs in the first inning. This was the first time in history two teammates had each hit two home runs in the same inning.

LEFT: Mike Cameron trots around third base after his first home run against the Chicago White Sox.
RIGHT: Cameron hits his third home run of the game.

Cameron was not finished. He came up again in the third inning against Parque and hit another ball into the stands for his third home run of the game. Two innings later, poor Parque was still on the mound when Cameron stepped into the batter's box for the fourth time. Sure enough, the Mariners' slugger hit home run number four.

No one had ever hit five home runs in a big-league game. Cameron hoped to be the first. In the seventh inning, he was hit by a pitch. In the ninth inning, Cameron drove a ball to the fence, but it was caught.

"I tried to go for it," Cameron smiled after the game. He had no reason to frown. He tied the record for most home runs in a big-league game.

LEGEND HAS IT

DID ANYONE EVER SEE 'BIGFOOT' AT A MARINERS GAME?

LEGEND HAS IT that they did—52 times! In 1986, Pete "Bigfoot" Ladd pitched in 52 games for the Mariners. It was not hard to understand how he got this nickname. Ladd stood 6′ 3″ and weighed 240 pounds. He had long, tangled hair, a bushy mustache, and enormous feet. He could be one scary dude! During the winters, when many players took long vacations, Ladd kept himself busy as a prison guard in his home state of Maine.

ABOVE: Pete Ladd thought the nickname "Bigfoot" was a good fit.

WHO WAS THE MARINERS' FASTEST-WORKING PITCHER?

LEGEND HAS IT that Felix Hernandez was. Hernandez joined the Mariners at age 19, but he often pitched as if he had no time to spare. In 2006, he took the mound in Seattle against the Los Angeles Angels of Anaheim and beat them 2–0. The game lasted just one hour and 51 minutes. It was the shortest home game in team history. In a 2008 game, Hernandez struck out the side on nine pitches. You can't work faster than that!

WHICH MARINER HAD A RECORD-SETTING START TO HIS CAREER?

LEGEND HAS IT that Alvin Davis did. Davis played his first game for Seattle against the Boston Red Sox on April 11, 1984. He hit a home run in just his second at-bat. He also reached base safely the next day, and the next day, and the next day. Davis continued to get a hit or a walk (or was hit by a pitch) in every game right through April and May. Finally, on June 8, the Cleveland Indians managed to keep the rookie off the bases for a whole game. Davis still holds the record for reaching base 47 games in a row to begin a career.

There was no prouder father in baseball than Ken Griffey Sr. when the 1990 season began. The 40-year-old outfielder for the Cincinnati Reds was the only man in the big leagues who could say his son was a big leaguer too. In fact, it was the first time in history that any active player could say that.

Ken Griffey Jr. was in his second season with the Mariners and having a great year as the team's center fielder. On August 29, Junior learned that a new left fielder was joining the team—his father!

Two days later, they were in the lineup together against the Kansas City Royals. Ken

Sr. hit a single up the middle in the first inning, and then challenged his son to match him. Ken Jr. did as his father told him, and hit a single to right field. In a game on September 14 against the California Angels, the Griffeys were at it again. They hit back-to-back home runs!

When the season ended, Ken Jr. had a .300 average. How did Ken Sr. do? He batted .377 in 21 games for the Mariners. The Griffeys played one more season together, in 1991. In all, father and son were on the same lineup card more than 50 times.

LEFT: The Griffeys have a father-and-son catch before a game in Chicago.
ABOVE: Once his playing days ended, Ken Griffey Sr. watched his son play as often as he could.

TEAM SPIRIT

The Mariners are always thinking of new ways to connect with their fans. They give away souvenirs and collectibles at the stadium. They hold special events for businesses and members of the military. The players support local charities and visit area schools. The Mariners run fun commercials on television that get fans excited about the team.

The Seattle area is home to a large Asian-American population. That's partly why the team looks for talented players from Japan and other Asian countries. Ichiro was one of several players who crossed the Pacific Ocean and became a star with the Mariners. In 2009, the team named Don Wakamatsu as its new manager. Wakamatsu was born and raised in the United States. His father was Japanese-American. That made Wakamatsu the first manager of Asian-American *descent*.

LEFT: Seattle fans appreciate when the Mariners give everything they've got.
ABOVE: Don Wakamatsu managed the M's in 2009 and 2010.

TIMELINE

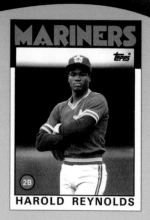

Harold
Reynolds

1977
The Mariners play
their first game.

1982
Gaylord Perry
wins his 300th game.

1987
Harold Reynolds leads the
AL with 60 stolen bases.

1979
The **All-Star Game**
is played in
Seattle's Kingdome.

1984
Alvin Davis is
named Rookie
of the Year.

1991
The Mariners have their
first winning season.

Bruce Bochte got
a hit in front of the
home fans at the
1979 All-Star Game.

Alvin
Davis

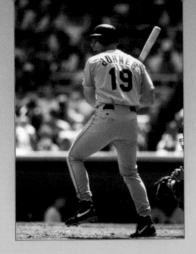

Jay Buhner hit 40 homers for the 1995 champs.

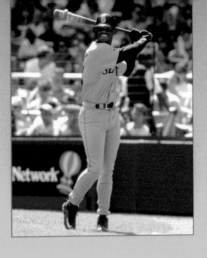

Ken Griffey Jr.

1995
The Mariners win the AL West for the first time.

1998
Ken Griffey Jr. leads the AL with 56 home runs.

2007
J.J. Putz records 40 **saves**.

1996
Alex Rodriguez is the first AL shortstop to win a batting championship in 52 years.

2001
The Mariners set an AL record with 116 victories.

2010
Felix Hernandez wins the Cy Young Award.

Felix Hernandez

Big Bang

The team's first home, the Kingdome, was demolished in 2000 to make room for a new football stadium. It took 5,800 dynamite charges to bring down the building, which fell in just 20 seconds.

Very Neighborly

In 2010, Franklin Gutierrez and Ichiro won Gold Gloves for their fielding skills. They played side-by-side in the Seattle outfield.

My Hero

Many teams scouted Felix Hernandez when he was a teenager. At 16, he picked the Mariners because his favorite player, Freddy Garcia, pitched for Seattle.

SINGLE SERVINGS

In a 2004 game, Raul Ibanez set a club record with six hits in six at-bats. Each of his hits was a single.

BAD START, NICE FINISH

In a 1993 game against the Boston Red Sox, Chris Bosio walked the first two batters he faced. He then got 27 outs in a row for a no-hitter.

MEN OF STEAL

Harold Reynolds holds the Mariners' record for stolen bases in a season with 60. Reynolds, Julio Cruz, Mark McLemore, and Henry Cotto share the record for steals in a game with four. Ichiro is the team's career leader with more than 400 steals.

WIN SOME, LOSE SOME

In 1993, the Mariners gave up 20 runs in a game against the Detroit Tigers. Six years later, Seattle scored 22 in a game against Detroit. Both are still team records.

LEFT: Franklin Gutierrez   **ABOVE**: Raul Ibanez

"Once I'm on my game, I can't fail. Give me one run and let's win."

▶ *FELIX HERNANDEZ, ON THE CONFIDENCE HE TAKES TO THE MOUND IN EVERY START*

"You can have fun, respect the game, and also play it hard. When you have that combination, you're going to put yourself in a position to be successful."

▶ *ALEX RODRIGUEZ, ON THE SECRET TO WINNING IN THE BIG LEAGUES*

"We have a responsibility of providing a good show for the fans. Getting hits and home runs is what they want to see."

▶ *ICHIRO, ON KEEPING FANS ENTERTAINED AT THE BALLPARK*

ABOVE: Alex Rodroguez   **RIGHT**: Ken Griffey Jr.

"I don't know if I can run any faster. I just ran as fast as I could."

▶ **KEN GRIFFEY JR.**, *ON SCORING THE RUN THAT SENT THE MARINERS TO THE 1995 ALCS*

"He was Mickey Mantle, Willie Mays, he was Ted Williams. He meant as much to baseball as any of those guys did."

▶ **HAROLD REYNOLDS**, *ON KEN GRIFFEY JR.*

"I had a million-dollar arm, but I wasn't thinking enough about how to be a pitcher."

▶ **RANDY JOHNSON**, *ON WHY HE DIDN'T WIN A CY YOUNG AWARD SOONER*

"The secret is for the starters to get you into the sixth or seventh inning."

▶ **LOU PINELLA**, *ON THE KEY TO PUTTING TOGETHER A WINNING PITCHING STAFF*

GREAT DEBATES

People who root for the Mariners love to compare their favorite moments, teams, and players. Some debates have been going on for years! How would you settle these classic baseball arguments?

THE 2001 MARINERS WERE THE BEST TEAM SEATTLE EVER PUT ON THE FIELD ...

... because they set an AL record with 116 victories. Seattle won 31 of its first 40 games that year. The club also had a 15-game winning streak and a winning record against every team in the league. Eight Mariners were picked for the All-Star Game. Ichiro was named the AL Rookie of the Year and MVP, but every player did his part. The Mariners were simply unstoppable that season.

THE 1995 MARINERS WOULD HAVE STOPPED THEM ...

... because they beat the mighty New York Yankees in the playoffs. Remember that the Yankees went on to win the pennant six of the next eight years—including beating the 2001 Mariners! The talent on the 1995 Mariners was amazing. Seattle had one of the greatest lineups in history with Ken Griffey Jr., Alex Rodriguez, Jay Buhner (LEFT), Tino Martinez, and Edgar Martinez. The Mariners' pitching wasn't bad, either. Randy Johnson went 18–2 and won his first Cy Young Award.

RANDY JOHNSON WAS SEATTLE'S ALL-TIME BEST PITCHER ...

... because it was almost impossible to get a hit off of him. The Big Unit terrified batters with his size and the speed of his pitches. He led the AL in strikeouts four years in a row, pitched a no-hitter in 1990, and was the first Mariner to win 20 games, in 1997. Johnson (RIGHT) was also an All-Star five times during his years in Seattle.

BOW TO THE KING! FELIX HERNANDEZ WAS BY FAR THE BETTER PITCHER ...

... because he pitched for a team that did not have great hitters. Yet Hernandez still won a ton of games—and a Cy Young Award of his own. Also, Johnson struggled with his control in his first few years with Seattle. Hernandez threw nothing but strikes from the day he joined the team. In his first seven seasons in Seattle, the team had a winning record just twice. But Hernandez went 85–67 during that time. King Felix wears the crown as the Mariners' all-time best pitcher.

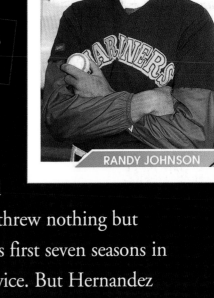

RANDY JOHNSON

The great Mariners teams and players have left their marks on the record books. These are the "best of the best" …

MARINERS AWARD WINNERS

WINNER	AWARD	YEAR
Alvin Davis	Rookie of the Year	1984
Ken Griffey Jr.	All-Star Game MVP	1992
Randy Johnson	Cy Young Award	1995
Lou Piniella	Manager of the Year	1995
Ken Griffey Jr.	Most Valuable Player	1997
Kazuhiro Sasaki	Rookie of the Year	2000
Lou Piniella	Manager of the Year	2001
Ichiro	Rookie of the Year	2001
Ichiro	Most Valuable Player	2001
Ichiro	All-Star Game MVP	2007
Felix Hernandez	Cy Young Award	2010

Alvin Davis

Felix Hernandez

Ichiro is congratulated by fellow Japanese star Kenji Johjima.

MARINERS ACHIEVEMENTS

ACHIEVEMENT	YEAR
AL West Champions	1995
AL West Champions	1997
AL Wild Card	2000
AL West Champions	2001

ABOVE: Randy Johnson won the Cy Young Award in 1995. **LEFT**: Bret Boone led the 2001 M's in home runs.

PINPOINTS

The history of a baseball team is made up of many smaller stories. These stories take place all over the map—not just in the city a team calls "home." Match the pushpins on these maps to the **TEAM FACTS**, and you will begin to see the story of the Mariners unfold!

TEAM FACTS

1 Seattle, Washington—*The team has played here since 1977.*
2 San Francisco, California—*Ichiro was named MVP of the 2007 All-Star Game here.*
3 Little Rock, Arkansas—*Glenn Abbott was born here.*
4 Bloomington, Indiana—*Phil Bradley was born here.*
5 Cleveland, Ohio—*The Mariners played in the 1995 ALCS here.*
6 Donora, Pennsylvania—*Ken Griffey Jr. was born here.*
7 New York, New York—*Alex Rodriguez was born here.*
8 Arno, Virginia—*Willie Horton was born here.*
9 Williamston, North Carolina—*Gaylord Perry was born here.*
10 Tampa, Florida—*Lou Piniella was born here.*
11 Valencia, Venezuela—*Felix Hernandez was born here.*
12 Kasugai, Japan—*Ichiro was born here.*

Phil Bradley

GLOSSARY

AL WEST—A group of AL teams that play in the western part of the country.

ALL-STAR—r A player who is selected to play in baseball's annual All-Star Game.

ALL-STAR GAME—Baseball's annual game featuring the best players from the American League and National League.

AMERICAN LEAGUE (AL)—One of baseball's two major leagues; the AL began play in 1901.

AMERICAN LEAGUE CHAMPIONSHIP SERIES (ALCS)—The playoff series that has decided the American League pennant since 1969.

COMPETITIVE—Having the talent and desire to win.

CY YOUNG AWARD—The award given each year to each league's best pitcher.

DESCENT—Family history.

DRAFT—The annual meeting at which teams take turns choosing the best players in high school and college.

EARNED RUN AVERAGE (ERA)—A statistic that measures how many runs a pitcher gives up for every nine innings he pitches.

GOLD GLOVES—The awards given each year to baseball's best fielders.

LOGO—A symbol or design that represents a company or team.

MINOR LEAGUES—The many professional leagues that help develop players for the major leagues.

MOST VALUABLE PLAYER (MVP)—The award given each year to each league's top player; an MVP is also selected for the World Series and the All-Star Game.

NO-HITTER—A game in which a team does not get a hit.

PACIFIC NORTHWEST—The coastal regions of Oregon, Washington, and British Columbia, Canada.

PENNANT—A league championship. The term comes from the triangular flag awarded to each season's champion, beginning in the 1870s.

PLAYOFFS—The games played after the regular season to determine which teams will advance to the World Series.

RETRACTABLE—Able to pull back.

ROOKIE—A player in his first season.

ROOKIE OF THE YEAR—The annual award given to each league's best first-year player.

RUNS BATTED IN (RBIs)—A statistic that counts the number of runners a batter drives home.

SAVES—A statistic that counts the number of times a relief pitcher finishes off a close victory for his team.

TRADITION—A belief or custom that is handed down from generation to generation.

TRIDENT—A tool or weapon with three prongs.

VETERANS—Players with great experience.

EXTRA INNINGS

TEAM SPIRIT introduces a great way to stay up to date with your team! Visit our **EXTRA INNINGS** link and get connected to the latest and greatest updates. **EXTRA INNINGS** serves as a young reader's ticket to an exclusive web page—with more stories, fun facts, team records, and photos of the Mariners. Content is updated during and after each season. The **EXTRA INNINGS** feature also enables readers to send comments and letters to the author! Log onto:

www.norwoodhousepress.com/library.aspx

and click on the tab: **TEAM SPIRIT** to access **EXTRA INNINGS**.

Read all the books in the series to learn more about professional sports. For a complete listing of the baseball, basketball, football, and hockey teams in the **TEAM SPIRIT** series, visit our website at:

www.norwoodhousepress.com/library.aspx

ON THE ROAD

SEATTLE MARINERS
1250 First Avenue South
Seattle, Washington 98134
(206) 346-4000
seattle.mariners.mlb.com

NATIONAL BASEBALL HALL OF FAME AND MUSEUM
25 Main Street
Cooperstown, New York 13326
(888) 425-5633
www.baseballhalloffame.org

ON THE BOOKSHELF

To learn more about the sport of baseball, look for these books at your library or bookstore:

- Augustyn, Adam (editor). *The Britannica Guide to Baseball*. New York, NY: Rosen Publishing, 2011.

- Dreier, David. *Baseball: How It Works*. North Mankato, MN: Capstone Press, 2010.

- Stewart, Mark. *Ultimate 10: Baseball*. New York, NY: Gareth Stevens Publishing, 2009.

INDEX

PAGE NUMBERS IN **BOLD** REFER TO ILLUSTRATIONS.

ABOUT THE AUTHOR

MARK STEWART has written more than 50 books on baseball and over 150 sports books for kids. He grew up in New York City during the 1960s rooting for the Yankees and Mets, and was lucky enough to meet players from both teams. Mark comes from a family of writers. His grandfather was Sunday Editor of *The New York Times,* and his mother was Articles Editor of *Ladies' Home Journal* and *McCall's.* Mark has profiled hundreds of athletes over the past 25 years. He has also written several books about his native New York and New Jersey, his home today. Mark is a graduate of Duke University, with a degree in history. He lives and works in a home overlooking Sandy Hook, New Jersey. You can contact Mark through the Norwood House Press website.